Soft & Fluffy Animals

Teddy Borth

Abdo
ANIMAL SKINS
Kids

abdopublishing.com

Published by Abdo Kids, a division of ABDO, PO Box 398166, Minneapolis, Minnesota 55439.
Copyright © 2017 by Abdo Consulting Group, Inc. International copyrights reserved in all countries.
No part of this book may be reproduced in any form without written permission from the publisher.

Printed in the United States of America, North Mankato, Minnesota.

052016

092016

THIS BOOK CONTAINS
RECYCLED MATERIALS

Photo Credits: AP Images, iStock, Shutterstock

Production Contributors: Teddy Borth, Jennie Forsberg, Grace Hansen

Design Contributors: Christina Doffing, Candice Keimig, Dorothy Toth

Cataloging-in-Publication Data

Names: Borth, Teddy, author.

Title: Soft & fluffy animals / by Teddy Borth.

Other titles: Soft and fluffy animals

Description: Minneapolis, MN : Abdo Kids, [2017] | Series: Animal skins |
    Includes bibliographical references and index.

Identifiers: LCCN 2015959003 | ISBN 9781680804966 (lib. bdg.) |
    ISBN 9781680805529 (ebook) | ISBN 9781680806083 (Read-to-me ebook)

Subjects: LCSH: Body Covering (Anatomy)--Juvenile literature. | Skin--Juvenile
    literature.

Classification: DDC 591.47--dc23

LC record available at http://lccn.loc.gov/2015959003

Table of Contents

Soft & Fluffy Animals

Animals have skin!

There are many kinds.

Some are soft.

Soft animals have **fur**.

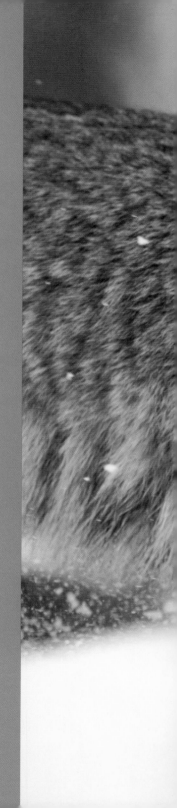

lynx

Fluffy animals have lots of **fur**!

muskox

Chinchillas have **fur**.

It is very soft to touch.

chinchilla

Some rabbits grow long **fur**.
It can be cut short. This does
not harm them.

Angora rabbit

An alpaca is soft. Its hair grows long. It is like **wool**.

alpaca

The Chow Chow is fluffy.

It looks fun to hug. Be careful!

It can be mean!

Chow Chow

Fur is good in winter. It keeps the Arctic fox warm.

Arctic fox

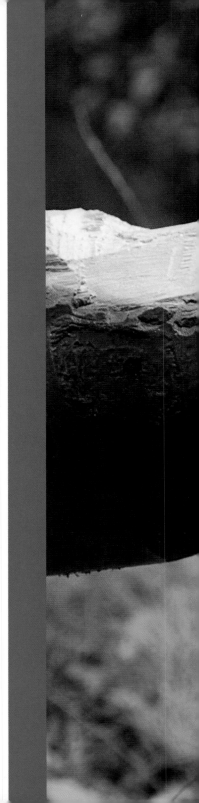

Beavers are soft. **Fur** keeps them warm in water.

beaver

Other Soft & Fluffy Animals

highland cattle

Pallas's cat

mink

silkie chicken

Glossary

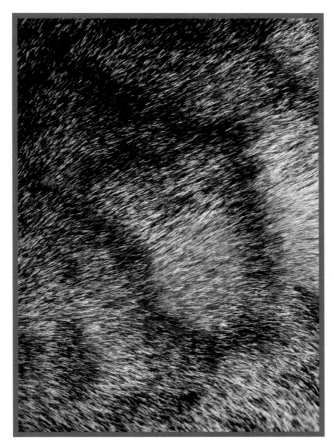

fur
the short, fine hair of certain animals.

wool
the soft, thick hair of sheep and some other animals.

Index

abdokids.com

Use this code to log on to abdokids.com and access crafts, games, videos, and more!

Abdo Kids Code:
ASK4966